D0351631

# *Fighters for Life*

3 8014 07017 0797

# Michael Rosen

## *Fighters for Life*
### SELECTED POEMS

Bookmarks
Publications

**STAFFS. LIBRARY AND INFORMATION SERVICES**

| 3 8014 07017 0797 | |
|---|---|
| HJ | 11-Sep-2009 |
| 821 | £7.99 |
| PENK | |

Fighters for Life: Selected poems
MICHAEL ROSEN

First published July 2007

Bookmarks Publications
London WC1B 3QE

ISBN 9781905192274

© Michael Rosen

Design and layout by rpmdesign

Printed by Cambridge Printing

Michael Rosen is a socialist, children's author,
broadcaster, performer and poet.

He is the Children's Laureate for 2007-9.

# PREFACE

A few thoughts on that word 'poem'.

Until the early 20th century there was general agreement in the western European and American traditions that poetry had either a regular rhythm or rhythm accompanied by a rhyme system. This overlooked the fact that various people had experimented with other forms, most notably those people who first translated the Bible's poetry into vernacular languages in sixteenth century Europe, the German poet and friend of Karl Marx, Heinrich Heine, who wrote a short cycle of free verse poems in the early nineteenth century, Walt Whitman, the American poet who wrote in a kind of Old Testament voice, the French bohemian Baudelaire who wrote what he called prose poems and the gay socialist Edward Carpenter, who at the end of the nineteenth century produced a free verse style all of his own.

In the early 20th century, a group of modernists led a campaign against the traditional forms and produced anthologies of free verse, seeing it as equivalent to the revolutionary changes that had taken place in painting and sculpture. Some of the most vocal of these avant garde poets were extremely right wing, but by no means all. American poets like Carl Sandburg and William Carlos Williams mixed their avant garde styles with socialist views and a few years later, the French surrealists produced their work as part of Communist, Trotskyist and Anarchist outlooks. By the time we reach the 1930s poetry had exploded into forms as wide ranging as pseudo film scripts, jazz sequences, sound poems and more. Poets have taught us that language is highly malleable. It doesn't have to follow the phrasing of sentences, paragraphs or regular verses. Playing with words is one way we can learn that we don't have to accept the world as it is given to us and that we can take part in changing it.

All this activity and diversity leaves some people stretching for definitions. I'm not sure that this is necessary. Whatever piece of print or performance comes in front of us, we can allow ourselves to enjoy it, contemplate it, respond to it on the basis of what we feel about it. Giving the form a name is an interesting exercise – it even has a reasonable role to play in helping us identify change in literature – but to make it an issue of value in itself is, to my mind, a dry, irrelevant formalism. That said, I've called these pieces of writing 'poems' but if you'd rather not, that's fine by me. Of all the many struggles we face, the matter of whether this or that bit of writing is a poem or not, is one of the least important.

All these poems were of course written in contexts mostly not of my choosing. One part of the environment where a writer usually feels that he or she can make choices, though, is in the matter of reading. It is in this way that we are always part of other kinds of writing on offer. This is not simply a matter of 'influence', but rather that writers are always in some kind of conversation with other writers, some long dead, some contemporary. I have a sense that though writers from the past might have a strong tug, it's the contemporary scene that is the more powerful. It encourages, legitimates and marks out territory within which you feel you can write. So, I can point to writers like Adrian Mitchell, Tony Harrison,

Benjamin Zephaniah, John Agard, Jean Binta Breeze, Roger McGough and Cecil Rajendra whose performances and books have played this role for me. My thanks to them.

But we've all written in the environment of clubs, theatres, schools, art centres and arts programming on radio and TV that have enabled us to reach audiences and make a living. And all the while, it's been the many varied struggles for freedom, justice, equality and emancipation that have created a context for us to intervene through poetry and performance.

What this intervention amounts to is a difficult matter to estimate. My own view is that the forms I've chosen to write in, in this selection, have enabled me to pick an angle, find a crack in the surface, crystallise a viewpoint or highlight a contradiction in received opinion. They're not solutions or programmes. They're not intended to close off thought or discussion. They're provocations.

I haven't updated any of the older poems here, so I've put in a date or note where it seemed necessary.

I would like to thank Mark Thomas of Bookmarks who has been one of the best editors I've ever had; Bookmarks bookshop for being a kind and helpful champion of my work and for publishing these poems; my father and late mother for being such loving parents, talkers, readers, performers and political beings; my brother for being a hilarious crap detector for his younger bro, my older children for not giving up; my dead son for living on, my younger children for their laughter and Emma for helping me get out of a pit. She says yes and no at exactly the right times.

Michael Rosen, London 2007

People in power
experts
say
Hang on;
Don't ask for too much
Times are tough
Don't take more than you earn
Hang on.

They say it this year
They said it last year
They'll say it next year
They say it every year

But every year
people in power
(who say Hang on)
get rich and stay rich.
They don't hang on.
They live for now
a rich now
and make others
live for a poorer now.
Year by year
these Nows
become Lifetimes
Rich Lifetimes and Poor Lifetimes

How many more poor lifetimes
will people put up with?

before they cut rich lifetimes
short –
once and for forever

---

1981

# How many

for Mordecai Vanunu

how many people
who know,
don't say?

how many people
who say,
don't say it all?

how many people
who say it all,
don't get heard?

how many people
who get heard,
get rubbed out?

how many people
who get rubbed out,
get forgotten?

how many people
remember the ones
they want us to forget?

If you need cheering up
you should try to make other people miserable.
If you're finding it hard running your own life
you should try to run someone else's.
If you think you're doing someone wrong
you should tell them it's their fault.
If someone asks you a question and you don't know want to answer it
you should draw their attention to the way they asked the question.
If you are unhappy that you feel weaker then someone
you should lie to them.
If you feel unappreciated
you should pour contempt on those you think as beneath you.
If you feel you've lost touch with what's real
you should try to make people believe in things that you don't believe in.
If you're not sure of the value of what you're doing
then you should denigrate what someone else is doing.
If you fear you've let someone down
you should tell them that they've let you down.
If you hate being grateful
you should do things that require other people to be grateful to you.
If you feel that you're not needed
you should tell people that no one thanks you for what you've done for them.
If you're afraid of hearing what someone thinks of you
you should tell them what you think they think of you.

If you feel weak
you should tell people what you think their problem is.
If you feel guilty
you should tell other people that they're trying to do bad
things to you

In a cartoon, at a time when some government or other was pleading with us to tighten our belts or go to war, or both, an overseer stood over a shipful of galley-slaves with a whip in his hand urging them on with: 'We're all in the same boat'. A bit like when the Lone Ranger turned to Tonto, his faithful companion from the Powatomie Nation, and the Lone Ranger says, 'Hey, Tonto, we're surrounded by Indians.' And Tonto says, 'How do you mean, "we", kemosabe?'

A family arrived and said that they had papers
to prove that his house was theirs.
— No, no, said the man, my people have always lived
    here.
    My father, grandfather…and look in the garden,
    my great-grandfather planted that.
— No, no, said the family, look at the documents.

There was a stack of them.

— Where do I start? said the man.
— No need to read the beginning, they said,
    Turn to the page marked 'Promised Land'.
— Are they legal? he said. Who wrote them?
— God, they said, God wrote them, look,
    here come His tanks.

## Triumph Sit-In, Meriden

It all came down to who owned the bikes.
We slept on the floor in the director's office
and in the morning they took us round the
factory to show us how they made them.
The line was still and half-finished bikes
were standing there. You might think
they had been parked there, but they were
too new and looking closely you could
see they were skeletons. They said that
the guy who had bought the factory was
just waiting to sell it off. A cowboy, they
said. And the bikes were sitting outside in the
yard. In wooden boxes, stacked high. The
steward who had spent his life asking for 2
and 3 and 4 per cent said that they had made
the bikes so now it was down to them to work
out what to do with them. We stood in the yard
and looked up at the stack. It seemed like this
was a brief time when we could think of them
in a new way.

In 73 BC
they crucified us in thousands
on the road to Rome
because we didn't want to be slaves.
They left us to die
so that we would learn
that we were wrong
for not wanting to be slaves.
But though we died that day
outside the town
we remember
We are not underground.

In 1649
we thought we could live
without kings
without lords
without judges
without priests
without masters
and we were going to dig
and sow and reap and share
but though they came and cut us down
we remember.
We are not underground.

In 1800
we ran from plantations
we ran from the fields
into the mountains and forests
When they came to find us

with their bayonets and muskets
some of us died.
But though they came and cut us down
we remember.
We are not underground.

In 1850,
they took our land
they killed the buffalo.
Though they massacred our people
we were always dangerous.
On the way to losing
sometimes we won.
Though they came to cut us down
we remember.
We are not underground.

In 1871,
we had a city
and we were surrounded
but we sat down
and made plans for the future
where we would run our own lives
run our own streets
run our own schools
run our own factories,
But instead they shot us and guillotined us
and they left us for dead.
Though they came and cut us down
we remember.
We are not underground.

We were napalmed for resisting
we were beaten for complaining

we were locked up for meeting
we were shot for marching
we were hung for refusing
we were raped for being who we are.

But none of this is forgotten.
None of this is buried:

Watch
Johannesburg
watch
Warsaw
watch
Belfast
watch
Santiago
watch
Detroit
watch…
…who knows where next
watch
where we have not forgotten
watch…
**us**
here
because
though they came and cut us down
we remember.

We are not underground.

---

January 1984

The black ticket collector was fifty.
When he swore to tell the whole truth etc
he looked at the Book like he knew it off by heart.

His lawyer said
the three white boys tried to run through the barrier
without paying.
When the ticket collector stopped them they started to
beat him up.
But he grabbed two of the boys, put them in the
broom cupboard
chased off up the road, caught the third
and locked him in the broom cupboard, too.

The boys' lawyer had an Oxford college in his mouth
and trundled out the law court patter:
— Rather than the events being as you describe
   I would suggest that you chose to assault these three
   boys
   I would suggest that you bore a grudge against them
   I would suggest that you took it upon yourself to attack
   them
   and I would suggest —
The ticket collector had never heard the I-would-suggest
   game
played by lawyers, believed by no one.
Furious, he called out:
— And I would suggest to you, sah,
   that as you was not present at de time
   you know nottin at ahl abote it.

The judge flipped up his glasses
— Very good very good. What d'you say to that?
And the lawyer said:
— ber ber ber ber
and went into a speedy decline.

And after much talking, the bomb stood up and spoke:
**Friends, I speak for civilisation and culture**
**I speak in the great tradition of standing up to**
**fascism**
**I speak for the rights of small nations**
**Abyssinia, Czechoslovakia, Poland**
**I speak in the name of —**
(here the bomb lowered his voice)
**I speak in the name of the six million Jews**

The room fell quiet
a roomful of our generals and leaders
all bearing emblems of peace and goodwill unto all men
all bearing fatigues and armour
blood-spattered from the battlefields
of Belfast, Port Stanley, Panama and Baghdad
all sweating and straining to keep control of their world
disorder.

One leapt to his feet.
**What can you do for us?**
And the bomb replied
**I can fly from the sky and find out your enemy**
**I can seek the culprit**
**pinpoint the armaments that deal out such pain**
**and misery**
**and,**
**like honey on fresh bread,**
**I can spread peace and comfort to all.**

Then our leaders spoke in agreement:
**we can select an enemy**

**we can choose a culprit**
**we can set your sights**
**we can show the world**
**that we can solve problems**
**we can win respect**
**we can keep power**
**we can keep power**
**we can keep power**

**Not so fast gentlemen**, said the bomb
**I am but one.**
**Before sending me on my mission**
**you must make many more like me.**

**No problem**
bellowed back our leaders,
each fresh from downsizing a hospital
from taking the slack out of pensions
from slimming down some meals on wheels
**no problem**
**we can make bombs**
**we can make bombs**
**go, do your best, make peace.**

And the bomb got up and left the room
and did what he has always done
whether it was in Guernica or Dresden
Hanoi or Baghdad
he found out, he sought, he pinpointed
someone driving a bus
someone bathing a wound
someone digging potatoes
someone scrubbing a floor.

And so it is that in the forests and mountains

victims become culprits
culprits become victims
culprits become victims
victims become culprits
and so it is that their generals and leaders
and our generals and leaders
send the starving victim-culprits
down to the shops to stand in queues
to buy guns and shells and tanks—
send them to clean each other off their farms and fields.

And all this time
their generals and leaders
and our generals and leaders
stroll on the lawns of international conference centres
explaining their position vis-à-vis the safe havens
yes, the safe havens,
not intending with that
to refer to their own skins
their own suits
and their own beds.

You generals and leaders in khaki, grey or light blue
you are not the solution
you are the problem
we will not choose between you
we will not say that one of you
cleanses more reasonably than another
that one of you brings peace in his briefcase or tank
we will not wave any of your flags
we will not sing any of your tunes
and we will not join your dance of death.

---

September 1995

He said, I can't stand it any more, it's doing me head in.
This place used to be like a village.
— What's the matter with it? I said.
— It's full of foreigners, he said. I love
    Walthamstow, he said, but I can't stay here.
    I'm going.
I wondered where but I said nothing. He didn't say
anything else, so I said, Where to?
— Spain, he said.

Detective Sergeant Farr said in court
on April 14th 1983
"It is highly probable that my closed fists
might have come into contact
with Mr Rose's face"
but Detective Sergeant Farr denied
deliberately punching him.

The Israeli government said,
It is highly probable that numbers of unnamed people
under the control of Israeli forces
went into certain camps full of people
with no exact address
and prevented them from continuing to live
but the Israelis denied deliberately helping to kill anyone.

The American government said
It is highly probable that pieces of metal
flew at very high speed out of the barrels
of what are commonly called guns
into the bodies of human beings
in the region known as the Honduras-Nicaraguan border
but the Americans denied being there deliberately.

The British government said
It is highly probable that the Argentinian battleship
the General Belgrano was not proceeding towards
the exclusion zone but was in fact proceeding
away from it, when a certain amount
of explosive material sank the ship and 650 people died,

but the British government deliberately denied nothing.

---

**1983**

"Detective Sergeant Farr said, 'It is highly probable that my closed fists might have come into contact with his face.' But he denied deliberately punching Mr Rose." — *Guardian*

## A Moderate

His Holiness the Pope says the sun goes round the earth
while the earth goes round the sun, say extremists in the
north.
In a war of propaganda, no one says what he means
I think the Truth, as usual, lies somewhere in between.

Roger was a lefty
lived in a basement flat,
taught slow learners,
wore a soft grey hat.

Roger was a theorist,
found time in between
to hit you with Althusser,
write articles for *Screen*.

Roger loathed marriage,
mortgages and taxis,
said we should soldarise
and always practice praxis.

He convinced some of his colleagues
that capitalism was shitty.
They thought long and deep
then fled the inner city.

There weren't many left
when the idea was floated
that Roger could do better:
Roger was promoted.

The comrades were troubled,
there was a bit of a friction.
He said he was a realist
he was facing contradiction.

To make his position clear
he tended to rant and hector.
Then Roger bought a suit.
Roger became an inspector.

He talked software, studied wines,
joined a gym, ran at night,
met Celia, bought the mobile
put it in his Samsonite.

Then one day
when Roger was resting,
he saw the future:
It said: Testing.

Marking, grading,
figures, tables,
checking, assessing
goals, labels.

He'd seen himself as
one of history's liberators.
Now he'd do it with
Performance Indicators.

He solemnly declared
he would never swerve
from giving the masses
what they deserve.

Marking, grading,
figures, tables,

checking, assessing
goals, labels.

Now equipped
with these ground rules,
he headed down town:
closed two schools.

To which plan he added
important features:
wrote a mission statement
and fired fourteen teachers.

Roger was amazed.
There were strikes and demos.
Roger was furious
he sent off memos:

'This is confidential
but I know the leaders
They're ex-friends.
Sack the bleeders.'

Roger was tough
Roger was thorough.
Roger brought rigour
to a Labour borough.

Roger brought success
Roger brought glory
and felt insulted
when he was called a Tory.

Well the Rogers of the world
don't always have it easy.
The protests swelled
he came over queasy.

Seems: just as Roger
got slicker and slicker
he put too much pressure
on his all-red ticker.

He packed his bags
he's not exultant
he's now what's called
an Education Consultant.

He travels around.
He helps. He advises
on how to live
with bigger class sizes.

Management teams
are keen to enlist him.
Roger remains as ever
useful to the system.

I got a letter home saying that Religious Education is compulsory. So I sent a letter back saying it isn't. They sent me a letter back saying but it is. So I sent them a letter back saying I've got the government papers saying it isn't and you're breaking the law saying that it is. And they send a letter back saying OK it isn't and we'll write a letter home to everyone telling them it isn't.

# *Republican Hate Poem*

May the King
lose his thing.
May the Queen
get gangrene.
May the Prince
be made into mince.
May the Princess
become an abcess.
May all the royals
come up in boils.
The odd Duchess or Duke
can turn into puke.
Same goes for a Knight
who should be reduced to shite.

In a school full of children and teachers called
Selima and Abdul and Shenazz a woman (white,
English) is talking in the staffroom about her father...
87 now, she doesn't see him, brutal to her when
she was a child, unspeakable stuff; he had been in
the army, in India, north-west somewhere, used to
tell them about what they did, he and the lads, like
two of them betting a packet of fags as to who
could shoot the old feller over there off his donkey.
One of them did. And the village. There was a
village. One day, one of the boys from the regiment
was shot. So that night, a group of them left the camp,
destroyed the village, killed everyone in it. Never
appeared in the records. Never reported. Back home,
that evening, I watch a reporter standing on the roof
of a house in Afghanistan next to a British soldier
firing at someone over there... the camera pans across
and takes in hills, houses, trees, dust. The reporter
explains that the soldier next to him is firing his gun
because the person over there is firing his. Legitimate
target, then. Tit for tat. The camera pans back: hills,
houses, trees, dust. For a second it's possible to see
that the person over there might think that the hills,
houses, trees and dust are his home. And the British
soldier is trying to kill him for wanting to defend it...
then we're back with the reporter urging us to think
about something he calls reconstruction.

Vultures cackled over our corpses:
their old dreams had taken shape:
we were carrion at last.

Vultures scoured and cleaned,
tidied up the carnage,
wanting no leftovers.

Vultures are looming now —
they hover over high-rise wrecks
and hungry queues,
hunting bodies,
screeching, 'Corpses? What corpses?
We're pretty boys!
Pretty boys!'

Parading as parrots,
they don't fool us —
because we are the leftovers,
the ones that poison vultures.

It didn't work out the way it's supposed to. The four of us on a platform. We were supposed to have given up. We should have learnt that being unconvinced is what counts for wise. But we're here. Shocked again. Coming out of our kitchens to say, if nothing else, everyone here is sick of the age-old cruelties. We should have noticed that history ended but we got distracted by some massacres. So we're here again. It didn't work out the way it's supposed to.

I

The London Institute of Applied Research Science
(L.I.A.R.S. for short)
has discovered that there are more parks
in middle-class areas than in working-class areas.
This shows, they say,
that working-class people
don't like parks.

II

The L.I.A.R.S.
have just completed a piece of research
which looks at two kinds of wounding:
cutting and striking.
They have discovered from watching
2000 hours of BBC News programmes
that striking kills
but cutting doesn't.
So, to save life
L.I.A.R.S. recommend
cutting hospitals and
banning striking.

III

L.I.A.R.S. think
that if you come from
an overcrowded home
then obviously it's a good idea
you should go to

an overcrowded school.
If children from big spacious homes
went to
overcrowded schools
they'd be very unhappy.
This proves that
things are best left as they are....

# *Who killed Blair Peach?*

with Susanna Steele

what's that on your hands, son?
what's that on your hands?

only a spot of blood, mum
only a spot of blood

how did it get there, son?
how did it get there, then?

must have been a nose-bleed, mum
must have been me nose

what's this down your coat, son?
what's this down your coat?

looks like blood an'all, mum
looks like blood an'all

that was never your nose, son
that was never just your nose

must have come from one of the others
must have come from one of our men

but it's all in your boots and socks, son
it's all in your boots and socks

all in the course of duty, mum
all in the course of me job

these stains will never come out, son
these stains will never come out

    they'll be put in the bin and forgot, mum
    they'll be put in the bin and forgot

they'll fix you up with new ones, son
they may fix you up like new
but I'll remember this, son I'll remember this:
you came home with blood on your boots
from a day of keeping the peace

---

1980

Blair Peach was a London school teacher killed while returning
from an Anti-Nazi League demo in Southall 1979. The six
police officers from the Special Patrol Group, who where
responsible for his death, were identified. As no individual
could be identified as the one who hit Blair, none of them were
found guilty.

I read this to some 4th year boys at Holloway School and a lad
at the back said, "Well, my dad's in the SPG and it weren't like
that". Two days later I got a phone call from the head telling me
that the police had been up to the school to object. The staff at
the school were great, though, and told them to get lost.

## Plaques

You who love history
you who love heroes
you who want to know about Great Men and Women
come to the walls of houses and palaces
and read the names of artists, reformers, inventors,
leaders, statesmen and entertainers.

You who are not great
when death was the meaning of your life
can find your names in the long lists on war
memorials.
They found room for you there.
But there is no room on the vast grey walls of new
blocks,
station forecourts, motorway piers or multi-storey car
parks
for the names of those who died on the sites.

Occasional national frenzy over mining disasters,
train crashes, and aeroplane explosions
fills the front pages.
A Royal death unites us in mourning
with grief-stricken polo players and multi-millionaire
show-jumpers
and their tears drown the sound of a bricklayer
tripping on a scaffold-plank and landing on his spine.

For him
no plaque.

"Plans to cut the number of health and safety inspectors must be reversed in the wake of an alarming rise in deaths on construction sites... Some 74 people have died on building sites in the past 11 months, 14 per cent more than in the previous 12 months, according to the unions Ucatt, Prospect and PCS."— *Financial Times*, 13 March 2007

# *Ariel Sharon Studies History*

"At a meeting in Chicago General William Sherman and other leading military men decided to break the 1851 Treaty of Fort Laramie and clear the plains of most of the Plains Indian tribes. They decided to put all the Plains Indians tribes onto two reservations, one in the north and one in the south, clearing a giant swath through the plains for the railroad. To make the tribes more ready to sign, they attacked village after village on various pretexts—sometimes for stealing cattle, sometimes for attacking homesteads. These military attacks were against the provisions of the Fort Laramie Treaty which pledged that violations such as stealing cattle and attacking homesteads would be punished in a court of law and not by military occupation."

---

This is a historical account found on a website explaining how the Plains Indians were cleared.
[from Washita on www.tolatsga.org/wasvo1b.html]

Lenny let it be known that he and his wife were interested
in finding out what all the fuss was about so would I
be so kind as to come to dinner where they and other
interested people would like to ask me some questions?
The university is nothing to do with Vietnam, they said.
Protest as much as you like but there's no need to do
all that occupying stuff and Enoch Powell is entitled to
speak for godssake. I think there was someone there
who drew unbelievably badly for the *Daily Telegraph*.
We don't see any connection between you complaining
about how we teach and the Americans bombing North
Vietnam. Protest as much as you like but do it peacefully
and don't blame us. Then Lenny's wife said, Lenny, we
left South Africa because we gave up on any peaceful
way out, do you remember? Lenny, she said, we know
that the only way Apartheid is going to end is through
armed struggle. Lenny sighed but got into trouble becase
when he became Lord Hoffman he forgot to tell someone
something important and General Pinochet was let off the
hook.

On the way there on the Victoria Line there was just one of them. I'd say about 14, short with it, and an old man's pot belly. He had some kind of accordion hanging from his shoulder. A small red piano accordion. On the way back, there were three of them and now I could see that he was in charge. He sat opposite me shunting coins from his tracksuit top to his tracksuit bottoms. His two boys came through the carriage with another red piano accordion. Exactly the same. These two looked about 9. They had polystyrene cups for the money, most of us reading newspapers. It was midday, a weekday, a Thursday, in November, between Pimlico and Victoria. They were trying out a daisy cutter in Kabul.

---

'With its use of the 15,000-pound "daisy cutter" bomb in Afghanistan, the United States has unleashed one of its most powerful weapons — billed as the world's largest conventional bomb. The BLU-82 combines a watery mixture of ammonium nitrate and aluminum with air, then ignites the mist for a huge explosion that incinerates everything within up to 600 yards. The shock wave can be felt miles away.'

World's Largest Non-Nuclear Weapon— *Associated Press*, November 6, 2001

Pinter lost his patience. Perhaps he was right, what with Kent and me being so polite with the petition, expressing this, conveying that, letting our feet rest on the Embassy carpet. Until then, their men had let their eyes wander over us. In a lazy way, with a smile or a shuffle of the hand, they let us know we were duff, they were subtle. Their job was to preserve a beautiful balance: letting the enemy know that it could be obliterated, but keeping this out-of-sight from friends. They weren't going to upset the design by letting their prisoner go. Not that anything was said. Pinter, I think, sensed it. He's good on silences, isn't he?

— Don't think we're going to forget this, you know, he shouted. They didn't blink. Neither did the Berlin Wall, I was thinking.

*Os gerissen zolste weren*, says my father
Don't say those things, says my mother
`ch `a` dich im loch*, he says
Don't say those things, she says
What's he to Hecuba? he says
The coat's nice. Wear it. They're wearing them like that,
she says
No job takes two minutes, he says
So? Did they like the coat? She says
Never believe a rumour till it's officially denied, he says
Leave him alone, he's tired, she says
Ah, the whirligig of time, he says
It's not burnt. It's crisp, she says
Your muscles stand out like sparrow's kneecaps, he says
Stalin must have been ga-ga, she says
*Genug is' genug*, he says
What's the use of a frying pan without a handle? she says
You look as sharp as a *matzo* ball and twice as greasy, he
says
Don't pick it, wash it, she says
My *zeyde* used to say: One match, you can break. Two
matches, you can break. A whole box of matches, you
can't break. That's a union, he says
My greatest horror was bedbugs, she says
Why don't you have some bread with your jam? he says
Seeing the dray horses slipping on the ice used to terrify
me, she says
What do you think this is, Liberty Hall? he says
No one else was defending us against the fascists,
so of course we joined, she says

*Tout va bien, Madam' de la Marquise*, he says
The lettuce needs cheering up, she says
What larks, Pip, he says
It's the way you're sitting, she says
Herrel Shmerel went to the races,
lost his *gatkes* and his braces, he says
You knew which ones were the doodlebugs, she says
So they call you *pisher*! he says

When they first started shelling out scholarships
round the old Empire,
David was their worst fear:
a biter of the feeding hand.
He spirited up the magically expanding Action Committee
that grew to engulf the bowler hats and gowns
of the university police.

In the occupation,
he was the first through the wrought iron gates
in his shades and chef's trousers;
caught by *The Times* photographer
as evidence that Malcolm X had hit the dreaming spires.

His girlfriend, Yvonne, was refused service
at Annette's the Hairdressers.
Six weeks of picketing didn't budge Annette:
there were going to be no blacks in her parlour.
So David proposed what he said would be
Britain's first sit-in against the colour bar.
The Ever-expanding Us agreed
that One Hundred would head down to Annette's
next Wednesday.
What with the picketing
Annette had got jittery
and arranged a hotline to the cops,
so we opted for a scattered assembly point.
We added ourselves on to the bus queues and sweet
shops.
The area saw a sudden increase in snogging couples.

Yvonne walked into Annette's for a cut.
The signal would be her reappearance at the door.
The scattered Hundred were holding the door in view
by glancing under their armpits, over newspapers.
The place was heaving
with normality.
Yvonne filled the doorway…

…and from the queues and the benches
the winos' rendezvous and lovers' embraces
we ran for Annette's.
In the rush
the hairdressers became the eye of a whirlpool.
20 got in, the rest sat down outside,
Annette shot out screaming
and came for us with the scissors.
I think the now urbane commentator
on American life, Christopher Hitchens,
got it in the skull;
in a matter of seconds
the wagons turned up, the warning read out
and we were soon being lifted
and thrown in the back.

On the day we appeared in court
we pleaded not guilty to obstruction
on the grounds that it was Annette
who was doing the obstructing.
As we were fined
another Hundred were facing Annette's scissors
as part of David's rolling sit-in concept.
For weeks, I was up to my eyeballs in David's concepts,

Malcolm X, Fanon, Lumumba and Cabral.
They started turning up in my dreams.
News from Jamaica in the early seventies
was that David had gone to the hills.
It was never necessary to ask what he was doing
in the hills —
it was enough just to mutter significantly
David has gone to the hills.
Then somebody said, David was in jail.
It was getting real.

In 1977, London *Time Out* listings
had David,
General Secretary of the Jamaican Workers' Liberation
League
speaking in Paddington.

I went.
He was till wearing shades
but now a suit.
I listened, waiting for the spark,
some new scheme,
an ever-expanding rolling, unstoppable whatsit,
that would release Jamaica and the world from
the machines that had crushed Hanoi and Prague.
No, it wasn't there.
Naïve white looney to think it would be.
Get real.

But as I sat puzzling about there the fizz had gone
he used the phrase:
*the peace-loving peoples*.

In fact he used it again and again.
The pages of *Soviet Weekly* and *GDR News*
(delivered to my parents,
once a fortnight by Bill on his bike).
flickered in front of me.
Smiling peace-loving peoples of Poland,
Romania and the KGB beamed at me.

At the end I said,
*- Hi, how you doing? Remem-*
And he said,
*— I meet a lot of people. Sorry I must go.*

My best friend knew the names for different kinds of apples, different kinds of birds, different kinds of cars, how to grow potatoes, how to paint a wall, how to make cement, how to get to Gillingham, how to make a go-kart, the whole of 'My nose is cold, tiddly pom' and scores of rhymes about bums and farting. We lived in each other's houses, climbed into the builder's store and made a den. We spotted a bullfinch in the woods next to the bypass and caught newts in the scraggy pond there. He wrote to me from Gillingham and Brixham, I wrote to him from Skenfrith and the Jura Mountains. He failed his eleven-plus. I passed it. He slowly stopped being best friend. For years I wrote about him, us and the go-kart, us and gymnastics on the sofa, us and Baldy, us and the tunnel, us and Old Man Adams. There was more to write: us and the tree house we never finished, the firework night where the whole lot blew up. One day, I tought, I'll bump into him and tell him how I've been acting out him and me and the go-kart for years in front of kids in schools. It's been my way of saying sorry that I had turned the thing over with him on the back. When I was forty I found out that he died when he was seventeen.

Poor countries need Relief
because they are poor

They are poor because
they have no money

Because they have no money
they have no food

Now some questions:

Why don't they grow food?
Because they are growing coffee, tea etc

Can they eat coffee, tea etc?
No

Why are they growing coffee?
To get money

Do they get the money?
No they give the money to us

And then they buy the food?
No the money is ours, they owe it to us

You mean they borrowed money?
Yep

To buy food?

No, to grow coffee, tea etc.

Why did they do that?
We told them to

Why did we do that?
So that they could be modern

Are they modern?
No, they can't afford to be

Last question:
Who is 'we'?
Banks

Conclusion:
They grow coffee, tea etc
pay banks money
starve

Proposal:
Short cut: next Comic Relief to be not for Africa
etc
but for banks… i.e. Bank Relief

They abolished exam courses. Instead, you enrolled for
a subject at school or at college and then part of your
course was a matter of guessing what the course ought to
be. So you read things and wrote essays and did practical
exams in topics that you thought the examiner might
examine you in. The best teachers and students were the
ones who guessed best – usually because the head of
the school or the department knew an examiner. This way
exam success was kept to elite institutions.

Another innovation was to reward students whose parents
hired private tutors. In the past, these kinds of families
were unfairly penalised. The parents might spend a good
deal of money on a tutor only for their offspring to do
rather badly in the end of year exam. However, in the end,
after several goes and a good deal more expenditure on
the tutoring, 'fails' like these were usually able to nudge
their grades up. To avoid this unfairness, a new system
was brought in whereby any student who had a private
tutor had their marks upgraded before the exam and not
after it. This way exam success would come to those who
most deserved it.

A useful advance was made when the authorities realised
that the apparatus for having marks for different subjects
was time-consuming and expensive. They brought in a
global mark that averaged out everything. What this meant
was that every child and student right the way through the
system was allotted his or her single grade. Parents would
know that their child, from the age of five, right the way

until they left formal education, was an 'A' or a 'B' down to 'F' for 'Fail'. Employers in particular found this much more useful than the old messy way of having to look across a range of grades, testimonials and candidate's letter and the like. The person in question was now quite simply a 'C' person or an 'E' person and everyone knew where they were.

The Politician believes in politicians,
Believes that when politicians talk it's as
if it's the whole people talking

Journalists believe in politicians
They quote them in their papers
They keep asking them what they think
They sit them in their studios to beam
their words into our lives

They even entice real people into asking
politicians some questions
And they reverently lay their answers
before us.

Out of sight of cameras
we make
we build
we celebrate
we mourn.
Throughout
we talk

But though
we have words
and voices
and skills enough
to run this show
we are forced to sit like galley-slaves
with all the power
and none of the control.

## Bad Language

I arrive at the school.
The headteacher says to me,
I'm so glad you could come
because you must understand
that the children here have no language.

That's funny, I say
I thought I heard quite a lot of noise in the playground.
They must have been saying something out there.

Ah well, no, not exactly no language, she says
bad language, not vulgar, mind –
anyway – you'll soon find out when you get in there.

130 seven and eight year olds come in
and we get along fine.
We have plenty to talk about
One boy tells me
he keeps his old Spiderman T-shirt tucked under the
mattress on his bed
so his mum can't get at it and use it as a duster

I do
'Down behind the dustbin
I met a dog called Jim
He didn't know me
and I don't know him.'
And one boy called out,
How do you know his name was Jim, then?
That had me beat.

Anyway, they leave,
and as I am leaving
the headteacher thanks me for coming to her school
and then explains to me, like many other places before
her, that this school has children
who aren't a patch on the children in the school up the
road.

That was the February when we could see that the reason why was not the reason why. The terrible man had been at his most terrible when they had been helping him. They said he was terrible because he took no notice when the world voted against him. So they took no notice when the world voted against them. This isn't terrible, they said. Then they did terrible things and took his country. This isn't terrible, they said. Waves and waves of us knew this before it happened; we had filled streets and parks and squares all over the world. Our coalition. They rang the newsmen. Ignore it to death, the newsmen said. But we walked on, and we walked on, strangers were friends.

# *Sharansky*

Remember Sharansky the freedom fighter?
A Jew in the Soviet Union
he said he was a refugee
in his own country.
Let me go to Israel, he said.
Let my people go.
He called out to the whole world
Has no one got the time to listen to us?
Will no one hear our cry for freedom?

In the end they let him go.

He arrived in Israel
and some people came up to him saying,
We are Palestinians
we are refugees in our own country
has no one got the time to listen to us?
Will no one hear our cry for freedom?

And Sharansky said,
Freedom? Freedom?
Sorry guys,
there isn't enough of that to go round for everyone.
Can't help you.

the society for saving unborn babies
said
they are very very much against contraception
they are very very much against abortion
and very very much in favour of dead mothers

1984

"Right class, look this way please. In this course on 'British Wars that weren't called Wars', so far we've looked at the Suez 'Crisis', the Northern Ireland 'Troubles' and the Falklands 'Campaign'. Today we're going to look at the Iraq 'Serious Consequences' of 2002.

Does anyone know where Iraq was? No Jason. Next to Wales is Ireland. Rasheda? Excellent. Yes, next to General Powell Gulf over here.

OK, so we know where Iraq used to be. Now let's go back to where it all began.

First, let's sort out the leading figures, they're coming up on your monitors now. And this is? No, Kurt, that's not Frank Zappa. That's Saddam Hussein. And this is? George W. Bush with his son and nephew who also both went on to become presidents. And this is? Anyone know? No, not one of the royal family. No, not George Bush's doctor. That's Mr Tony Blair. He was prime minister of this country. I had rather hoped you'd know that, class.

Now, moving on. One more major player in the 'Serious Consequences' war: at this time, the organisation that all the countries of the world belonged to was called the…? The…? No, not Manchester United. It was the United Nations. Which, as we know, following the 'Serious Consequences' war, became the USN, with it's first president? Yes, George Bush's niece.

Now to what the war was about. OK, George W. Bush and Tony Blair said that it was about something called 'Weapons of Mass Destruction'. Why were these a problem? Yes, Sophie? No, it wasn't because Bush and Blair had them. Anyone else? No, not because Ireland had them...oh you meant to say Israel. No, Israel having Weapons of Mass Destruction wasn't a problem either. Well, I'll tell you: it was because President Bush and his Mr Blair said that Saddam Hussein had them and this was a danger to world security.

Daniel asks, 'What about the Soviet Union?' I don't follow you. Oh I see, you mean was it a danger to world security when the Soviet Union had Weapons of Mass Destruction? No, it wasn't because of what was called 'Mutually Assured Destruction'. That's to say, both sides in the Cold War knew that they could wipe each other off the face of the earth. In the case of the 'Serious Consequences' conflict, it was different. American and Britain could wipe Iraq off the face of the earth but Iraq couldn't do it back. That's why Saddam Hussein was a danger to...er...world...erm...security. Yes.

Moving on...to what some historians call the real causes.

What did Iraq have that would turn out to be very useful for the rest of the world? Gordon? Yes, they did have plenty of sand, but I'm thinking of something else. Oil. Who knows what oil was used for? No one. Well, oil was this thick black syruppy stuff, which when it was processed could be used to run cars, trains, factories, well, pretty nearly everything. The Serious Consequences conflict was just one of many Oil Wars stretching back to the Suez Crisis and stretching forward to the Caribbean Revolt and the Saudi Collapse.

Well, Sophie, now that there's no oil left, that's not what

people fight about now, is it? So, we know that the conflict wasn't about sand, and we know that President Bush and his Mr Blair wanted Saddam out of the way.

How did the do it? Very good, Ahmed. Yes, the Iraq Inspectors. Well, they weren't called that exactly. They were called 'Weapons Inspectors'. Though it was true that the only place they went to look for weapons was in Iraq. And the point was: President Bush and his Blair said that if the inspectors found weapons, they would take Saddam out. Stop giggling. No, they didn't mean 'take out', like that Samantha. And what did the inspectors find? You've got the document in front of you. I must admit I find it quite hard to remember the exact words myself...here you are...insufficient negative indications that might suggest or contradict that the intention or preparation for a conflict involving WMD's which might be construed as being evidential was not materially proven given the contraindications from hitherto reliable sources.

That's the crucial sentence. It was this sentence that gave President Bush the vital evidence he need to invade Iraq. And what did Mr Blair do? Absolutely right, Martin. He sent in the Green Goddesses.

By the way, before we finish today, does anyone know what became of the Iraqis? Does anyone know how many were killed? How many died? No, that's OK,  you see, it was a trick question, because just as in the Vietnam War that we did last term, no one knows.

OK class, don't forget to salute the Stars and Stripes as you go out. Dismiss."

---

written in 2002 on the eve of the big demo

I've got a passport number, a driving licence number,
a national insurance number, a tax reference number,
a bank account number, a council tax bill reference
number.
In the passport office I am a British citizen
in the airport I am a European
on the council form I'm white.
Him
he's a migrant, an immigrant, an illegal.
She's on a work permit, he's an asylum seeker
I don't need to worry, that's not me
I'm indigenous, I'm local
I'm native, I'm national
I'm not watched
by Migration Watch.
I'm not subject to being suspect
because I'm subject to being a subject.
They've invented who I'm supposed to be the same as.
They've invented who I'm supposed to be different from.
And it's all to keep me from thinking
that the fact that we're different
is what makes us the same.
It's the fact that we're different
that makes us the same.

When they do war
They forget how to count.

They forget how to count
And that's how they do it.

They come
They kill
They kill
They go
They give us
No numbers
Of the ones they kill.
No numbers
No names
They disappear them
They vanish them
It's how they do it.

They come
They kill
They kill
They go.

Names are deleted
Names are un-counted
Bodies are un-included
Faces are un-remembered
That's how they do it.

They come in
They flush out
They mop up
They take out

No numbers
No names
No names
No numbers

And it's worth it, they says.
It's worth it, believe us,
It's worth it, believe us.

Of course it's worth it
It's so cheap
It's so neat
If you forget how to count.
If you forget the numbers
If you forget the names
If you forget the faces
That's how they do it.

But we're counting.
Watch us
We're counting
Listen
We're counting.
And
We count.

Two men came and sat in my kitchen,
opened their suitcases on the table,
took out files and plastic folders and
asked me if I knew anyone who might be
able to front a show they were producing.
I suggested Alex, musician, story-teller,
writer, entertainer…(they seemed interested)…
…and presenter of a radio programme called
Black Londoners.
He's black, is he? said one of the men.
Yes, I said.
Does he try to bring it in? he asked.
What? I said.
Being black, he said, being black. Does he
try to bring it in?

The bus goes on and it's full and it's leaving and it's
laughing and it's going on and it's morning and it's
evening and it's in Punjabi and it's daytime and it's
full and it stops and it's suspicious and it starts and
it's in Ibo and it's shouting and it's shopping and
it's rapping and it's lit up and it's dark and it's shove-up
and it's crying and it's squealing and it's in Dutch and
it's braking and it's in Geordie and it's at the station
and it's skint and it's full of babies and it's full of men
and it's going on and it's past the Vietnamese café and
it's past the tyre depot and it's past the silver car and its
chauffeur and it's waiting for Sinatra to start up and it's
in patois and it's chips and vinegar and it's past the
park and it's full of football and it's a bellyache and it's
full of jokes and it's scared and it's in Arabic and it's
back from school and it's pushing and it's raining and
it's ripe armpits and it's tranks and it's angry and it's
full of yesterday and it's riding under the lights and it's
fucked off and it's the smell of oil and it's pissed and
it's combing and it's kissing and it's packets of rice and
it's cassava and it's over the canal and it's the baby's
bottle and it's over the railway and it's under the cranes
and it's in the shadows of the palaces in glass and it's
in Albanian and it's bleach and it's the homework in
late and it's spuds and it's the hijab and it's shoulders next
to backs next to fronts and it's revving and it's too late
and it's too early and it's not enough and it's going on
and it's on time and it's dreaming and it'll get there
today and it'll get there tomorrow

The acoustics engineer on the train from Manchester
to Birmingham told us about the future:
— You might be going past a shop and its database
    would inform you that you had bought a shirt there nine
    months ago and surely wasn't it time you bought a new
    one?
    They would know when you ran out of milk and when
    enough people in the street had run out too, the
    electric milk float would be round delivering milk to your
    door.
In a voice full of wonder, he said:
— They would know all your desires.

Laskey said:
— What if you wanted goat?

I think he was still with the milk. I said that
I thought Goat Enterprises would have picked up on the
time when you bought suede shoes and perceived that
you were a potential goat person; you had a goatish
profile.
Nadine from Goat Enterprises would call:
— Hello Laskey. Nadine from Goat Enterprises here.
    Pardon me for calling, but we noticed that you
    bought some suede shoes last week. Have you ever
    considered drinking goat's milk?
And you, Laskey, would you say:
— Nadine, you don't have to be part of this. Let's get
    away together.

And Nadine would say:
— Are you asking for a brochure on weekend breaks at one of our traditional Goat Farm Experiences?

It was in an office that I overheard a woman saying that she hated council flats and tower blocks. But it wasn't the architecture, it was the people. Out there, on the other side of this window, her line was that it was bad. People were bad. In here we are OK. But if you were with her on your own, meeting her, one by one, then for her the others in here were bad too. So we were all bad. That only left her who was good.

In 1963 in one of the lifts on Goodge Street Station there was an ad for Jaeger cardigans.
There was a man and a woman in a loose clinch.
They were looking into each other's eyes.
I thought it would feel good to have love like that. That you could look right into each other's eyes. That would be good. Underneath, it said, 'We're in love in Jaeger.'

— Michael Rosen, can I ask you some questions?
— *Yes, of course.*
— Are you a Jew?
— *Yes, I am*
— And where is your home?
— *London*
— What is your country?
— *I'd like to think I'm of no country and of all countries but the law says that my country is the UK*
— Has it always been your country?
— *Yes*
— And your parents, and grandparents and great grandparents?
— *Well, if you're going back that far, we start talking about places like Poland, Russia and Romania*
— So is Israel your homeland?
— *No, of course not*
— So, will you ever go to live in Israel
— *No, of course not*

— *Thank you for asking me these questions. Next person please. Can I ask you some questions?*
— Yes, of course
— *Are you a Jew?*
— Yes, I am
— *And where is your home?*
— London
— *What is your country?*
— The UK
— *Has it always been your country?*

— Yes

— *And your parents, and grandparents and great grandparents?*

— Well, if you're going back that far, we start talking about places like Poland, Russia and Romania.

— *Is Israel your homeland?*

— Yes, of course.

— *So will you ever go to live in your homeland?*

— No, of course not.

He didn't lie.
He hasn't lied
He hasn't been lying
He wouldn't lie
He couldn't lie
He wouldn't have lied
He couldn't have lied
There was no chance that he was lying
It was so unlikely for him to have lied
that we can say that he certainly did not lie
A man in his position could not have countenanced
the possibility of lying
Familiar as we are with the kind of person that he is
it is unthinkable that he would have been so reckless
as to have lied
In the light of him being a person who knew only too well
that it was he in whom we all placed the utmost trust, it
is beyond belief that he could have betrayed that trust by
lying
It really cannot go unsaid that the fact that we always
regard him as one of us is essentially the reason why we
find it unthinkable that he could have lied.
If it is the case that he lied, then in order to prevent people
thinking that this is a normal state of affairs, we should
really do what we can to make clear that he isn't one of us
We are now moving towards an exceptionally dangerous
situation in which millions of people believe that it is
perfectly possible for their leaders to lie

There could come about a situation in which millions of people think that it is impossible to have people who lead them who don't lie.

## War Breaks Out

Who knows about war? says the editor.
I do, says the minister.
I'll talk about why we need war now.
You're on camera 1, says the editor
I do, says the defence analyst
I'll talk about the thickness of defence armour.
You're on camera 2, says the editor
I do, says the retired general
I'll talk about troop manoeuvres
You're on camera 3, says the editor.
I do, says the historian
I'll talks about how we won the Battle of Hastings.
You're on camera 4, says the editor.
I do, says the doctor,
I'll talk about skin and blood and bone.
Not today, thanks, says the editor.

## Songs of the Dead I

From Iraq

We have no mouths
We evaporated
You don't see the holes in the ground where we were put
We are the unfound
We are uncounted
You don't see the homes we made
We're not even the small print or the bit in brackets.
You see less of us than you see of the dust
You see less of us than you see of the wind
Because we were somewhere else,
because we lived far from you,
because our minutes, hours, days and years did not last
as long as yours,
because you have cameras that point the other way,
because you talk about other people…
…Of that moment when we went
you can't even say you missed it.

If you go into other people's countries
and bomb them
they will bomb you.
You can call them what you like
You can tell us that our cause is noble
You can tell us that they're evil and we are good
But the rule remains:
If you go into other people's countries
and bomb them
they will bomb you.
You can tell us that you've flushed out the troublemakers
You can tell us that you've neutralised the flashpoints
You can tell us that you've sown the seeds of the future
But the rule remains:
If you go into other people's countries
and bomb them
they will bomb you.

## *Songs of the Dead III*

From the three trains and the 30 bus

Thank you so much for lying
when we asked you why.
Thank you so much for not listening
when we said, don't go.
Thank you so much for ignoring us
when we said, don't shoot.
Thank you so much for carrying on
when we said, get out.
Thank you so much for taking no notice
when we said, this'll make things worse.
Thank you so much for making it impossible
for us to go on saying thank you.

Our mothers and fathers
fought the thugs who came to torment them on the
streets.
They organised in their places of work against magnates
who were pouring milk down mines, shooting miners
killing Afghans and hobnobbing with Hitler.

They fought the Nazi Axis
with the planes and tanks and machines

and millions wept

Such a tale of separation of lovers, of brothers, of sisters,
of children, of husbands, fathers or mothers
such a fall of streets, towns, countries and continents
had never been known.

So much – so quickly
so much killing, plunder and ruin, so much energy, so
much power
so many brains, so many hands, making machines to
break machines.

Out of the blood and oil, out of the iron and steel
out of the fires and infernos, the burnt wastelands,
the pits and heaps of broken bones –
our mothers and fathers came together

and with them came the oil-owners, iron-owners,
steel-owners, fire-owners, inferno-makers, waste-makers,
home-breakers.

None of *them* had been in the sewers of Warsaw
they weren't on Main Street Hiroshima
they weren't eating rats in Leningrad
they didn't queue in the markets or at Auschwitz
they didn't set light to their own roofs
to stop enemies sheltering under them
they didn't stand at the beaches and lathes
beg for water, wash pants, boil a potato, or pick apples.
They didn't even lift the gold they hoarded.

This gang of dictators, commanders, chiefs and bossmen
discuss how the power that lies in the earth of the Earth
shall be shared,
and commandeer the men, women and children
on the earth of the Earth to get it.

There is no trail of destruction of living things,
no trick, no system, no pain, no breaking of bodies
no sickness, paralysis or torment
no hunger, fear, fever or cold
that these men will ever hold back
from leaving in their path

who dies for them?
who died in Budapest? Haiphong harbour?
or on the streets of Derry?
who died in the football stadium of Santiago?
in the Sabra and Shatila camps?
or in Tiananmen Square?
who dies for Rio Tinto Zinc
the Chernobyl Nuclear Power Project
and the Grand Consolidated Gold Mine?

who gets maimed

making, building, washing, digging and cleaning?
who falls, who drops before their time?

People who have nothing
people who start every day with nothing
but their heads and bodies
people who hope to have strength enough
to work enough
to get food enough
to build up their strength enough
to work enough –

fighters for life.


Against this force of world work
a cellarful of worldwide chiefs and operators
rule and penetrate
every street corner, vineyard, barrack and mine
the fish-nets, stables and broom-cupboards,
the beaches, hospital bays and stoves.

Fighters for life, makers of life, lovers of life
we need ways of coming together and holding together
where we fight for life
where we make and love that life
or we will be called up for the armies of destruction
for the cellarful of worldwide operators
and so live to die.

If all we had to do was
simply become more and more skillful
then we could admire and applaud .
the craft and brilliance
of the engineers and fence-builders
the plumbers and welders
the fitters and designers
the draughtsmen and the architects
the planners and the chemists
who made the Concentration Camps
the clever places they were

1976

At Easter things got pretty serious at our school.
Before the event there was an enormous amount
of hymn practice and when we sang:
'There is a green hill far away
Without a ciy wall…'
every year they told us
that it doesn't mean
that the green hill hasn't got a city wall.

Then we went back to class and they told us the story:
those horrible Jews getting him
and poor old Pontius Pilate not knowing what to do
and then hammering nails through his hands and feet
then afterwards with him wondering down the street
and Thomas sticking his fingers
into the bleeding hole in his side…
the whole thing was pretty serious and pretty messy.

I felt a bit bad about those Jews.
I mean I didn't think *Zeyde*'d do a thing like that
and I kept my head down in class
in case anyone thought I was in on it too.
But Jesus was a Jew as well
I didn't see why I should get it in the neck.

As for Pontius Pilate, I found out later
he was really like any other ordinary Roman psychopath
and loved stringing people up
especially Jews.
Strange story –
a bit too violent for kids, I should think.

Cecil Rhodes, John Hawkins, Captain Cook,
Oliver Cromwell, Lord Clive, Lord Codrington
In a cast of millions
in the
GREAT ILLEGAL IMMIGRANT SHOW

Gasp with amazement
at
Cecil Rhodes' frantic grabbing of African Lands.
Be stunned to silence
as you watch the Matabele forced
to sign away all rights to anything
of where they live.

Gape with wonder
at
John Hawkins
breathtaking kidnap of African people
and then before your very eyes
sell them like horses.

You'll hardly believe your ears
listening to Captain Cook
helping his diseased sailors to survive
the hard job
of plundering the South Seas

Sit riveted in your seats
as
Oliver Cromwell

the founder of our parliament
forbids the Irish to speak Irish
and then
exiles them from Ireland.

You'll think your eyes deceive you
as
you watch the Great East India Company
milk the richest nation in the world
till its fields lie dry
and millions lie dying from hunger.

Hold on to your seats
as you are transfixed
by
the noble Codrington in Barbados
trying to breed slaves
to cut his sugar cane
and clean his palace.

All these and many more:
wiping out Indians in America,
Aborigines in Australia,
Scots in Scotland
in
THE SEVEN GREAT PLUNDERS OF THE WORLD
IN
THE GREAT ILLEGAL IMMIGRANT SHOW.

---

1982

A group of eight year olds
follow me into a room.
3 boys, 3 girls.
'Let's move the table,' I say.
We all move the table.
'Who's going behind the table?' I say.
'Me,' says one boy –
'Gettaway from the girls,' he says.

After 8 years alive in this world
we have taught him to be at war
with half the people in the world

A woman broke into the House of Commons
today
during the Third Reading of the Nationality Act

She shouted from the floor of the House:

'Who the bloody hell do you think you are?
sitting there in the same seats
as people who once ran the slave trade,
starved Ireland and India by the million
led unarmed Africans to be slaughtered
in the First World War,
practiced armed terror in Malaya,
Cyprus and Kenya,
created hate across the globe
between peoples you once ruled…

and now you sit cooly invent
First Class Brit
Second Class Brit
Third Class Brit.
You are about to unleash
thousands of First Class Brit Policeman
on to any visibly
Second or Third Class Brit
to check his or her right
to visit a doctor
to stand, sit, talk, walk, or breathe
in the presence of an officer of HM Police Force.

Every day of your lives
you enjoy the services

of people who have settled here,
just as you enjoyed them when you settled
in their countries.
Your grandparents die in their arms
your babies are brought into the world by them
your bus-journeys are made safe by them
your hotel stays are catered by them
your fancy meals are made by them
they make some of your cars, cakes, clothes and houses

Yet not one of them sits in here
contributing to your civilised discussion
concerning their fate –
you who think you are the representatives of the people
are inflicting democracy on the unrepresented.

I pray that one day you have to stand
in a police station
on the street
in a doctor's surgery
or in the middle of a job of work
and plead
and plead
the right to be
a human, here, now and equal.'

The woman was led away
and later charged with
disturbing the peace.
She pleaded, 'I hope I'm guilty of that.'

---

1982

# Enough

I've heard enough about Eichmann and Himmler
Heydrich and Bormann
— sadistic maniacs etc etc
I've heard enough about Hitler
— cunning diplomacy, magnetic oratory etc etc

Just tell me
who gave them the money to start the thing off.